LONDON
INTERIORS

This book is dedicated to the memory of
David Hicks

LONDON INTERIORS

BOLD · ELEGANT · REFINED

BARBARA & RENÉ STOELTIE
Foreword by DAVID GILL

Flammarion

ACKNOWLEDGMENTS

We would like to express our profound gratitude to all those who have assisted us in making this book and especially those who have received us with such sincerity and warmth.
In addition to acknowledging the help of the owners and occupiers of the exceptional houses shown in these pages, we wish to offer our special thanks to Sera Hersham, David Gill, Francis Sultana, and Jean-Jacques Wattel, without whom we would have been unable to translate the magic of London into words and images.

Text and Photo Styling
Barbara Stoeltie

Photographs and Layout Design
René Stoeltie

Copyediting and Proofreading
Lise Connellan

Typesetting
Cyprien Godin

Color Separation
New Goff, Ghent

Printed in Ghent, Belgium by New Goff

Simultaneously published as *La Magie de Londres*
© 2013, Fonds Mercator, and the authors, Brussels
www.fondsmercator.be

English-language edition
© Flammarion, S.A., Paris, 2014

CONTENTS

ROOM AT THE TOP
Christopher Gibbs

"For many are invited, but few are chosen" (Gospel of Saint Matthew, 22: 14) could well be applied to the career of antiques dealer Christopher Gibbs—only a few exceptionally gifted dealers like himself ascend to the top of their profession. Born into a wealthy, upper-class family, Christopher studied at Eton and at the Sorbonne, and has traveled the world extensively since his early youth, now dividing his time between an apartment in London and several properties in Morocco. It would seem that he has inherited his gregarious nature from a grandfather who was born in Devonshire, spent part of his youth in Spain, and died in Venice!

During the Swinging Sixties Gibbs was an undisputed style icon and one of the leading figures of the Chelsea Set—a few well-bred and strikingly attractive young dandies who defined the new fashions, ruled the day, and invented the Peacock Style. Gibbs's famous friends were Mick Jagger, Keith Richards, and Brian Jones, and in his bachelor apartment on Cheyne Walk one would rub shoulders with the artistic and eccentric jeunesse dorée of the era. His home served as a backdrop for a scene in Michelangelo Antonioni's film *Blow-Up*. It was only a matter of time before "Chrissy" opened an antique store on Sloane Avenue and ended up doing what he did best: decorating extraordinary houses for the well-to-do and the odd eccentric, and filling their rooms from top to bottom with exceptional furniture, paintings, and objets d'art.

How would one describe the "Gibbs Look" without being excessive in one's praise? How does one find the right words to focus attention on Gibbs's unique talent for combining objects from various periods and different origins, and his flair for creating interiors that are elegant, relaxed, and a hundred percent "chic"? In his very private apartment in The Albany—one of the most prestigious addresses in London, built between 1770 and 1774 for Viscount Melbourne by Sir William Chambers, and refurbished in 1802, after the departure of the Viscount, as a set of sixty-nine bachelor flats by Henry Holland—Gibbs has proved that his style is at the origins of "country chic." Chez Gibbs, antique furniture, exotic textiles, a Victorian brass bed, a stuffed panther, engravings, letters, and piles of books fill the modestly proportioned rooms in a rather nonchalant way. After all, this is the home of an antiques dealer who has opened the eyes of his clients—not to say the world of interior design connoisseurs—to the beauty of antique, faded velvet, rickety Georgian wing chairs, oversize period sofas, and larger-than-life family portraits and busts. He has emptied castles and manor houses to fill flats and apartments with unique treasures from the past. Perhaps this is why he has chosen to retire—"far from the madding crowd"—to the heart of London, surrounded by his favorite objects, with a good book and a glass of wine. Christopher Gibbs is truly a lucky man.

LIVING IN VAUXHALL

David Gill

A TROMPE L'OEIL VIRTUOSO
Roy Alderson

It would take only a quick glance at the front door of the late Roy Alderson's London terrace house to realize that this was the home of a remarkable artist, for very few would have had the skill to paint a door with arabesques that looked deceptively like stucco ornaments.

Roy was a famous trompe l'oeil artist and all those confronted with the stunning technique that enabled him to decorate walls, furniture, objects, and even a London taxicab with an illusion of three-dimensional ornaments, would be surprised by his almost childish pleasure in pulling the leg of the viewer. Let us not forget that the art of trompe l'oeil is the art of deceiving the eye and Roy superbly walked the thin line between real and fake, making his own home the showpiece for his exceptional talent.

Visiting Roy's world meant stepping through a spectacular entrance decorated with wildly undulating rocaille elements and walking into a drawing room where nothing was what it seemed, including the dachshund in the corner. Having discovered the intricate pen and ink decorative technique on furniture from the Regency period—an art that originated from India, his favorite vacation destination—Roy loved to cover bookcases with fake black and gold intarsia. Also, having spent many summers in Italy, the cradle of trompe l'oeil, he painted the walls of his bathroom with views of the Tuscan countryside. To complete the visual trickery he hung a chandelier that he designed himself, made of carved wood and decorated with dragons' heads, from the ceiling of the living room. Today we still wonder at Roy's ability to turn his modestly proportioned, Victorian terrace house into a "palazzo" by the simple addition of copies of neoclassical statues *d'après l'antique*.

Roy Alderson's undisputed pièce de résistance was the decoration of the Italianate garden at the back of his house. Originally the garden was nothing more than a bleak courtyard confined between high, whitewashed brick walls. Roy took out his paint and brushes, and metamorphosed the place into a splendid *giardino* filled with real and fake plants, a flight of steps with a balustrade partly real and partly trompe l'oeil, and the plaster statue of a Greek goddess. This is a perfect marriage between the second and the third dimensions that epitomizes the work of a great artist who succeeded, with incredible mastery, in combining truth and artifice.

A POSTMODERNIST ARTIST'S COCOON

Duggie Fields

DESIGN FOR THE FUTURE
Seth Stein

After graduating from the Architectural Association in London, Seth Stein immediately started working at the firm of Richard Rogers, a giant in his field and co-architect of the world-famous Centre Pompidou in Paris. The next in line to offer Seth a job was Norman Foster, the architect of Berlin's rebuilt Reichstag and equally one of the great names in his profession. With such an impressive portfolio, Seth could have easily applied for a job at another major practice, but in 1996 he felt that it was time to start his own business in the UK capital under the name Seth Stein Architects.

In the same year Seth bought a Victorian coach house to provide enough space for both his business and his growing family. Once again he succeeded in proving that his theory of making the most of a limited floor plan was the right approach. Stein's restoration and conversion of this old building was both surprising and innovative because he created the impression that he had taken absolutely no notice of the existing building in his restructuring and the redistribution of the various spaces.

The originality of Seth's private house—apart from the fact that he has created an inner courtyard, a large living room with a glass wall that gives onto this courtyard, and a concrete cylinder that houses the elevator—lies in the fact that he has juggled with the different volumes. On the newly built large walls there is enough room to hang large paintings and the spiral staircase in the living room has taken on the impressive stature of a contemporary sculpture.

Seth is keen to stress that the old coach house did not offer him a lot of room for expansion because there was very little to expect from an old building that used to provide room for only a few horses, a coachman, and a carriage. In the end the only elements he kept were a tiled wall—the wall of the former stables—in what has become the dining room and the beams of the former hayloft in which he has installed the master bedroom and bathroom. To complete the transformation of this Victorian coach house into a modern home he has also added concrete and parquet floors, and a fireplace, glass walls, and sliding doors.

The spiral staircase and the "rosa mexicano" colored wall in the kitchen bear witness to the architect's admiration for the genius of Le Corbusier and Luis Barragán. However, further proving that he is no follower and has his own, distinctive style, he has introduced an inventive mix of contemporary design and "vintage" items such as the fifties lamps of French designer Serge Mouille, early furniture by Marc Newson, chairs by Arne Jacobsen, a Knoll table, and, in the bedroom, the famous Bibendum chair designed by Eileen Gray. Never forgetting that he is a minimalist at heart, he has allowed only a painting by Mark Francis, a pumpkin, and a scale model of a vintage airplane as decorative objects.

"A house does not need clutter, just architecture!" is Seth's motto, an assertion that has been the architect's golden rule throughout his career.

A TRIBUTE TO THE EIGHTEENTH CENTURY
John Howard Gaze

The late antiques dealer John Howard Gaze did not care a bit for the era in which he lived, and those who knew him well admired his determination to turn his back on the twentieth century by deliberately choosing to live in a Georgian house filled with period furniture and paintings. John was a passionate dealer who specialized in Russian antiques and in his tiny but very exclusive shop in one of the passages that links Piccadilly and Jermyn Street, he sold icons, precious Fabergé Easter eggs, delicate objets d'art, bronzes, and fine porcelain. In the evening he went home to his house in the less fashionable East End to close the shutters, light the candles, and enjoy a unique atmosphere that was reminiscent of the interiors in William Hogarth's famous engravings.

When John bought his house in Spitalfields, the East End was still plagued by poverty and crime, but slowly the "Neo-Georgians" took over the area and meticulously restored the former silk weavers' houses that had been badly neglected by generations of indifferent Londoners. World-famous artists Gilbert & George had bought a near-ruin to house their living quarters, studio, and collection of Arts and Crafts furniture, and ceramics and paint guru Jocasta Innes had been one of the first to sing the praises of the former "Hospital Fields." Soon the East End became "the place to be" for the cream of the artistic intelligentsia, and people like John quickly joined the circle of enthusiasts who were busily scraping away layers of dirt and flaking paint, replacing missing bits of paneling or a period fireplace, and raiding the auction rooms and antique stores to get hold of a wing chair, a Georgian drop-leaf table, or a Queen Anne bookcase. In John's house every room was filled with eighteenth-century furniture, objects, and paintings, and because of his trained, discerning eye and his talent for composition, his home ended up looking like a window onto the past.

John Howard Gaze left this life almost unnoticed. A few years before his death he had moved out of his house in Spitalfields to install himself in The Albany, in the legendary apartment of the late style icon Baroness Pauline de Rothschild. A more opulent style of decorating had won him over and plaster busts, mahogany bookcases, and a ceiling painted by Ricarco Cinalli had chased away the Hogarthian simplicity. *Panta rhei* (everything changes). All that remains today are the pictures of the little Georgian house in the East End.

AN ARGENTINIAN IN SPITALFIELDS

Ricardo Cinalli

THE ART OF RECYCLING
Keith Skeel

It is common knowledge that the London antiques dealer Keith Skeel has a strong aversion to minimalism; if one day he should be in need of a motto that fits his congenital need for accumulation like a glove, "More is more" would be the perfect choice. Keith simply adores the sight of heaped-up pieces of antique furniture and objects of every style and origin. This perhaps explains why he cuts a single figure among his more conservative colleagues.

Keith is also known for his habit of buying antiques in large quantities. The clients who flocked to his former warehouses in the heart of Islington to buy a mirror or a chest of drawers would find it hard to make a choice from the dozens of examples on offer. In a very short time he had succeeded in turning his Camden Passage store and storage rooms into an impressive Aladdin's Cave.

Skeel has always been proud of his modest origins, although he does not make an issue of his difficult start as a dealer in the Bermondsey and Portobello antiques markets, where he sold his "goodies" (he preferred to call them "schmutter, baloney, and tat") from a trestle table on the sidewalk. In the end his efforts were rewarded and his booming business finally enabled him to acquire Loudham Hall, a superb eighteenth-century country house in Suffolk, which was built for an illegitimate offspring of King Charles II, and an imposing brownstone in a top New York location.

From the very beginning Skeel acquired a reputation for dealing in "eccentricities"—unusual antiques like witch balls, stuffed animals, and oversize furniture. Such objects would never escape his keen eye when on a buying trip, and soon his store and homes overflowed with items that would not have looked out of place in the Kunstkammer of an eccentric collector.

Like all antiques dealers, Keith also has "attics" that contain odd "bits and pieces"—scraps of furniture, sculptures, crockery, and the incidental porcelain statuette without a head. Keith claims that while undergoing an extremely painful session at his dentist he had a strange vision of a room whose walls were decorated with a myriad of broken items. On his return home he decided that the basement corridor of his home would be the perfect place to give shape to his hallucination. For weeks on end a craftsman patiently nailed and glued fragments onto the walls of the underground passage leading to the garden. Today the surreal "grotto" is painted white and Keith Skeel is more than pleased to have been able to dispose of what antiques dealers fear the most: the unwanted and the unsalable!

A NEOBAROQUE INTERIOR

Danielle Moudaber

A NEOBAROQUE INTERIOR
Danielle Moudaber

One of the favorite quotations of artist, designer, photographer, and interior designer Danielle Moudaber is a statement by the world-famous British photographer Cecil Beaton, who once said "Be daring, be different, be impractical, be anything that will assert integrity of purpose and imaginative vision." On entering her apartment in the heart of Kensington one understands immediately that Danielle has followed Beaton's advice literally and that her breathtaking decorative scheme is a three-dimensional tribute to the power of audacity.

Danielle bought her one-bedroom ground-floor apartment in 2004, but when four years later she had the opportunity to buy the apartment upstairs she did not hesitate a second. Her flamboyant, creative spirit needs space— lots of it!—and her passionate compulsion for larger-than-life furniture, decorative objects, and contemporary art can flourish only in generously proportioned rooms. Small wonder that her craving for a "total look" has been influenced by the interiors of gurus of art deco style Louis Sue and André Mare, and that she also cites the exuberant creations of the late Valerian Rybar and the much missed Tony Duquette as sources of inspiration. By following the principles of these giants of interior design, nothing in Danielle's neobaroque world is ever too big or too powerful.

Like most artists endowed with exceptional talent, Danielle Moudaber gets away with murder. Her powder-blue walls, her giant plaster moldings (Dorothy Draper, eat your heart out!), the serpentine dining-table-cum-bar-on-wheels, the oversize, deep-buttoned sofas, chaises longues, and forties stucco wall lights, and the black labyrinth that has been handpainted on the white floorboards, right in the center of the drawing room, are clearly not for the fainthearted. Danielle knows how to walk the tightrope between the masculine and the feminine, and how to combine her stunning photographs of the statues of the Roman Stadio Olimpico with rococo plaster ornaments and neoclassical cornices.

Born in Africa and raised in Lebanon, Danielle cherishes her childhood memories and she is keen to admit that she has been much influenced by a domestic life that revolved mainly around an intensely blue swimming pool. Hence her love of a "watery" shade of blue and sun-flooded rooms. They form the perfect background for the spectacular "organic" staircase that leads to the upper floor, the fantastic furniture and lamps designed by Mark Brazier-Jones (with whom she created unique pieces for her clients), and the frivolous "wedding-cake" decorations on the paneling of her bedroom.

Danielle has been described in French as "*une artiste décoratrice*" and this is not an overstatement for she is, quite obviously, not only an interior designer but also, and chiefly, an artist. Her interiors are "environments," dreamlike creations, and much closer to a fairy-tale world than to reality. Cecil Beaton was right. We have to be daring and different. And Danielle Moudaber is living proof.